little caterpillar dreaming

• *a story* •

jo eden law

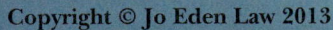

National Library of Australia
Cataloguing-in-Publication Entry

Eden Law, Jo 1973-
Little caterpillar dreaming.
ISBN978-0-9945292-0-6

Book Design by Jo Eden Law

All photographic images provided by Getty Images. For full credit details of the contributing photographers please visit **www.joedenlaw.com**

For the little caterpillar
in all of us.
x

PROLOGUE

It was daybreak, and the sky that was shrouded in a blackened veil courageously revealed its luminous truth. In the blink of an eye, the illusion of darkness faded into light as life committed to another day of intention.

A parade of ants made their way home after a successful forage, a beehive hummed with activity as the morning duties were in motion, and just beyond, down a winding road, a little caterpillar made her way into the mysterious, auspicious world.

And so it was, as it was always meant to be.

PART ONE

WELCOME TO THE WORLD

The little caterpillar heard the echoes of a chant as she opened her eyes for the first time.

"Let this caterpillar take her fate and live a life of whole. For nothing matters more in life than the truth within one's soul."

As the chanting faded away, the little caterpillar wrestled within a gelatinous casing that enveloped her. She thrashed and kicked feverishly until she finally poked through a crack. As she continued to push through the fissure, she suddenly felt an enormous pull. It sucked her body through like a vacuum, leaving her gasping for breath.

"Wellllllcommmmme…tooooo…theeeee…Worrrrrld littllllle onnnnne." A slow, deliberate voice percussed above her.

The little caterpillar lay exhausted and bewildered, yet she sensed a tremendous feeling of love.

"Aaarrrrre youuuuu alllllllriiiiight?"

A hot, humid gust of breath walloped her face. She could see a long spindly stalk, with an eye on the end, quizzically swaying around her. The little caterpillar nodded.

"Yooooou arrrrre heeeeere."

The little caterpillar wondered where "here" was as she watched the creature straighten up its spiral shell then continue on its path.

"*Carrrrrpe diiiiiiem!*"

The little caterpillar tilted her head and furrowed her brow.

"*Carrrrrpe diiiiiiem* means seiiiiiize the daaaaay."

"*Carpe diem,*" the little caterpillar whispered.

From that moment the little caterpillar understood that there was more to life than just her and that there must be a reason for being. The truth was, the little caterpillar was a unique piece in the divine puzzle, and her life mattered beyond comprehension.

"Soooooo looooong for nooooow."

And with that the curious mollusc glided away.

Life is a gift; seize the day.

Little Caterpillar Dreaming

As the days passed the little caterpillar took the words of the snail to heart. She embraced her new life and her surroundings with great curiosity. Everything she experienced was new and exciting, especially watching the butterflies dance around the milkweed grove.

The little caterpillar would get lost in her dreams for hours, wondering how she could learn to fly, just like them. She felt an intrinsic connection to these winged beings, and even though they looked completely different, they were actually the same.

"OUTTA MY WAY!" a brash little voice screamed as the air filled with the most putrid stench. The little caterpillar moved just in the nick of time as a giant ball of dung rolled past her.

"What the hell do ya think ya doin?" The dung appeared to squeak with an air of superiority. Out stepped a greasy dung beetle adorned with golden incisors and an impressive trio of long, pointed horns.

"Dreaming of flying?" The little caterpillar quivered feeling quite intimidated by the aggressive bug.

"Ha! Dat's the best joke I've eva hoid!"

"It's not a joke. It's my dream."

"Yar a right punk, aren't ya? Whadda ya think I am, Stupido? Dreaming of flying? Ha!"

"Everyone has dreams, don't they? Well mine is to fly… just like a butterfly." The little caterpillar fluttered her arms, attempting to prove herself and convince them both.

"OK, now ya getting on my noives. Ya don't know who ya talking to, does ya?"

"No, I'm sorry I don't. Who are you?" the little caterpillar asked innocently.

"Who am I? Who am I?"

The little caterpillar nodded.

"I'm a beetle of a higha orda. A sophisticated beetle on a mission. A beetle that doesn't give time to the likes of ya or ya cockamamie dreams. It's against da beetle code."

"The beetle code?"

"See ya don't even know what it is, does ya? Well it doesn't matta. Da beetle code says, dere's no such thing as dreams. Get ya head outta the clouds. *Capisce*?"

The little caterpillar shrugged.

"Undastand this. Yar a measly catapilla. I'm a *superiore* beetle. We are different kinds and dat's all dere is to it."

"But why does it have to be that way?"

"Dat's the beetle code and dat's just da way it is!"

"But what's life without dreams?"

The dung beetle flicked his hand towards the caterpillar with a flagrant disregard as he rolled his giant ball of dung away.

Jo Eden Law

Little Caterpillar Dreaming

"Just a measly caterpillar? A different kind? A life without dreams?" The little caterpillar felt her lip quiver and her body wilt as a wave of loneliness washed over her. She looked to the sky to find some comfort and as though an unspoken wish was granted, a group of butterflies glided above waving their magnificent wings.

The little caterpillar was enchanted by their grace and tremendous skill, they made flying look so effortless. She studied them carefully as they playfully danced, then a thought sparked.

"Aha! I need wings!" The little caterpillar rejoiced.

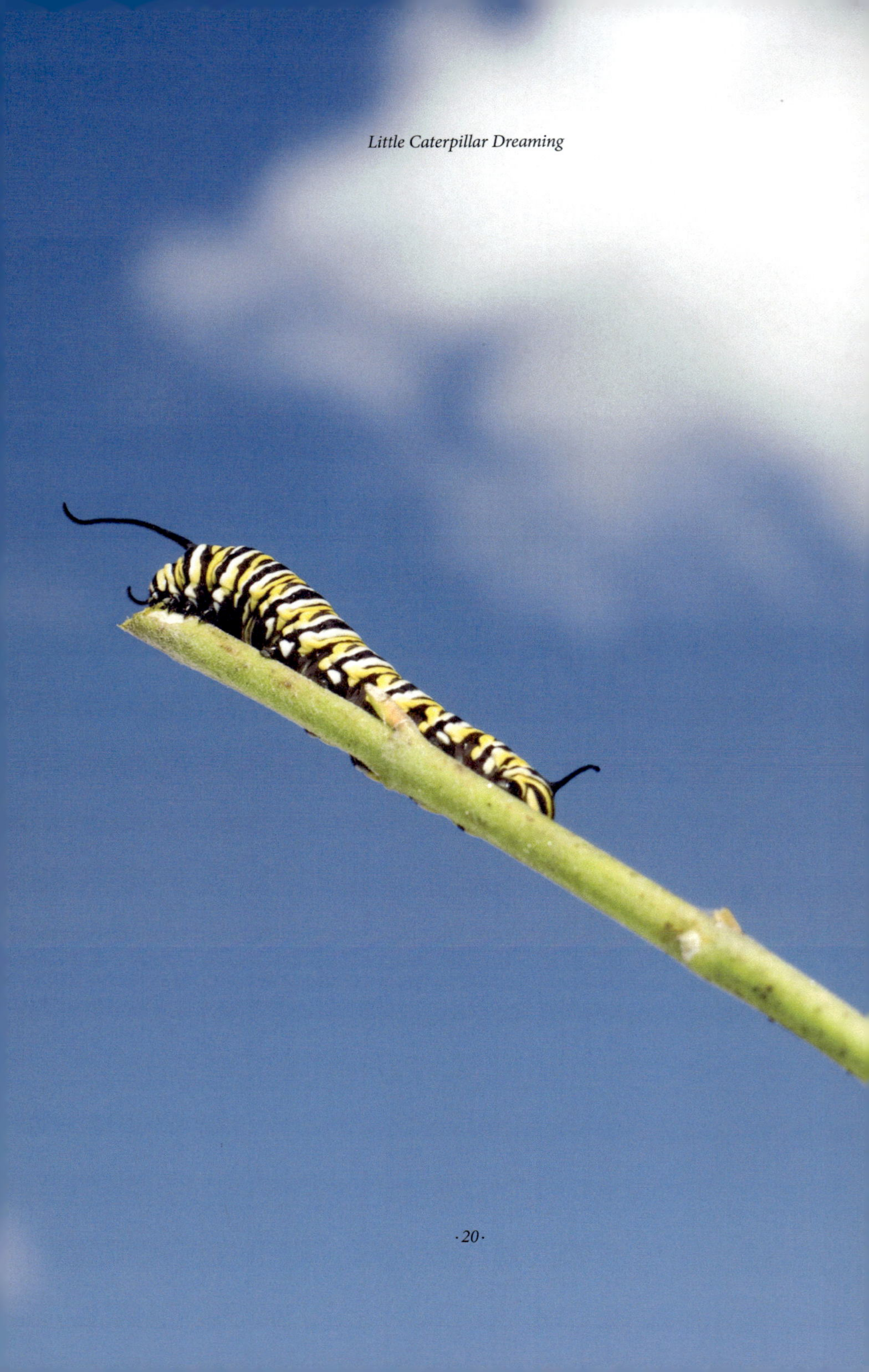

Jo Eden Law

The little caterpillar rummaged around the milkweed grove and found the perfect leaves and vines to construct her belief in dreams. She measured, folded and shaped the leaves then eagerly fastened them to her body. Like a tipsy moth the little caterpillar readied for take-off.

As the little caterpillar sprinted up the stalk of the milkweed, her mind was left unwilling. Her body wobbled at the weight of the artificial wings, which felt awkward and cumbersome.

She flapped her arms for dear life, swaying this way and that way, and all the while she focused on the things she wasn't able to do. She couldn't run fast enough, she couldn't flap her arms hard enough, she couldn't keep herself steady enough. And as the negative thoughts reverberated she stopped abruptly at the end of the stem as though she had hit a brick wall.

Time after time she wouldn't take the leap.

"Why can't I do this?" The little caterpillar whimpered. She slumped down in such a pout that she fell backward against a branch, breaking her wings into pieces.

"The beetle was right!" the little caterpillar muttered beneath her breath as the tears threatened to burst.

The little caterpillar was completely absorbed by her failure. She felt so angry and confused that she curled into a ball and wished she could disappear. In fact she was so wrapped up in her own world that she couldn't care less what was going on around her. She was not concerned that a rustling sound was coming from within the grove. She did not hear the twigs cracking under the sound of footsteps. She did not sense something moving closer and closer towards her.

Jo Eden Law

PART TWO

THE TRUTH IN SILENCE

When the little caterpillar finally looked up she saw that standing before her was a vibrant green grasshopper majestically wrapped in an ochre-coloured robe.

"Can I help you?" the little caterpillar offered cautiously as she clung to her mangled wings.

The grasshopper placed its hands together in front of its chest and bowed its head. It said nothing.

"Please sit down," the little caterpillar said, gesturing to the leaves and the branches surrounding them.

The grasshopper slowly nodded in acceptance, then sat down cross-legged in front of her, making the most beautiful sounds with every movement.

It then sat in silence.

"I beg your pardon!" blurted the little caterpillar. "My dream was to fly and I just can't do it. I'm nothing but a measly caterpillar. A failure. And to make matters worse, I've ruined my…my wings." She picked up the tattered wings to show the attentive grasshopper and then started to sob uncontrollably.

The grasshopper remained silent and the little caterpillar continued to weep, then she wailed, then she howled. She carried on and on until she had no tears left. At that point the grasshopper spoke.

"Grasshopper says, she who believes will fly, will. She who believes won't fly, won't."

Jo Eden Law

Little Caterpillar Dreaming

The grasshopper then stood up, bowed gracefully towards the little caterpillar and melodically sauntered back into the grove, leaving the little caterpillar uncertain.

Maybe the grasshopper is right, she thought, I WON'T fly.

The little caterpillar chose to believe "won't", rather than "will". She knew it would be easier to dream about flying rather than actually doing it. She knew it would be easier to justify her failure than to pursue accomplishment.

And as time crept on its petty pace, the little caterpillar dreamt and ate, dreamt and slept, while life continued to pass her by. She was becoming the caterpillar she never wanted to be.

Life is what you make it.

Little Caterpillar Dreaming

One day, after a heavy downpour, the milkweed grove was soaked from root to tip and the leaves were laden with mirrored droplets. The little caterpillar was going about her lazy routine of dreaming, eating and sleeping when she unwittingly glanced at her reflection.

She couldn't believe the sight of herself and was nearly bowled over in shock. Her eyes were dim and murky, her cheeks were gaunt and sallow, her arms were flaccid and weak and her body was gorged like a flatulent bovine.

"How could I let this happen to myself?" The little caterpillar thought as she scrutinized herself from head to toe.

Meanwhile, below on a nearby branch a mantis took perch.

"Well, well, well, *bonjour* my delicious, fat, little caterpillar. You look utterly scrumptious today, good enough to eat!"

The little caterpillar was snapped out of her thoughts and instinctively hid under a twig. She could feel a chill in the air.

"Ha, ha, ha!" bellowed the voice most unkindly. "You're an embarrassing little creature, aren't you? Do you honestly think your oversized body can't be seen? I knew you were fat and lazy, but dumb too? Oh, ho, ho, my perfect prey!"

The little caterpillar shook like a leaf. She could hear the voice echoing throughout the grove, but it was impossible to see where the evil lurked.

Jo Eden Law

"Don't fret, my chubby little cherub, I am not planning on devouring you today. I would rather take care of the hopeful first and leave the hopeless until last. Yes indeed, I will wait and save you for a special feast, maybe my last supper. Yes, that sounds marvellous! Perhaps I will invite my nearest and dearest to join the festivities; there will certainly be enough of you to go around."

The little caterpillar shivered.

"Until next time, *Mon Cherie*!" And with that the dark voice faded into an eerie silence.

Hours passed before the little caterpillar had the courage to move. The dark voice continued to resonate deep within.

"An embarrassment…fat…lazy…dumb…hopeless."

At first a few words lingered, but as time passed the words burgeoned like a patch of poisonous mushrooms. The dark voice had no mercy. It was relentless.

The ego thrives on fallacy.

Jo Eden Law

Over the next few nights the little caterpillar barely slept a wink. She couldn't get the evil voice out of her mind and started to believe everything it said. It took every ounce of energy to face the day.

"Another day," the little caterpillar huffed as she rolled out of her leaf and inched her way down to the bottom of the grove.

At that very moment a luminous fairy moth frolicked above her. The beautiful creature danced on the currents of the wind. Flitter, flutter, pirouette, plummet, loop and soar.

The fairy moth had a radiance that glowed like a beacon in the night. However, the little caterpillar was oblivious to the light above her; she was blinded by darkness.

"Hello, little one. You look rather sad. How can I help you?" the fairy moth asked with a lilt of a feather.

The little caterpillar looked up towards the sky. All she could see were the burnt edges of a winged being.

"Unfortunately you can't. I'm hopeless," the little caterpillar muttered as she slipped into a soppy puddle of mud.

"Well that just happens to be my specialty, helping hopeless little caterpillars find hope," the fairy moth soothed as she lifted her into the air and placed her on solid ground.

"You see, I have brought you something quite hopeful indeed. All you have to do is find your true purpose and I will grant you any wish your heart desires."

"I don't believe you, I'm afraid," the caterpillar sighed. "Hope is for the fairies."

"Well what a serendipitous moment. I happen to be a fairy!" The fairy moth fluttered in jubilation.

She pulled out a sparkling wand and waved it around like a conductor in a symphony orchestra. "Happy Birthday, Daisies!" she exclaimed. She closed her eyes, took a deep breath, and dotted the ground below. Within an instant, a twinkle of light sparked from each dot and a perfect row of daisies sprung from the ground.

The little caterpillar was in awe.

By the time the little caterpillar regained her wits about her the fairy moth had vanished. She double-checked the ground to confirm what her eyes had just witnessed, and there the vibrant daisies swayed knowingly in the breeze.

Faith is a sacred confidence in the intention of life.

PART THREE

THE BUSYNESS OF LIFE

"Excuzzze me! Buzzzy, buzzy, buzzy! " A busy little bumblebee whizzed by, narrowly missing the caterpillar's head. "No time to chat! I'm incredibly buzzy," the bee droned as she flew passed again.

"I'm so buzzy, buzzy, buzzy! I don't even have time to THINK of stinging you, let alone ACTUALLY stinging you. That's seriously buzzy!" The bee hummed on. "Anyway, you look like you have a mind full of bumble. What's up? Make it quick!"

"Ummm, OK, how do I find my true purpose?" the little caterpillar asked.

A peppery aroma that lingered from a distant bouquet of freesias distracted the bumblebee. She whizzed around chaotically trying to locate the origin of the scent, and then returned to the caterpillar, unsuccessful and slightly annoyed.

"Hummmm. Sounds like nonsense to me! Maybe if
you get buzzy like me, you won't have to worry about it!"
The bumblebee buzzed as she took flight again, then
whizzed back and forth in record speed. She appeared
to be very busy indeed.

"What keeps you so busy?" the little caterpillar asked,
feeling exhausted just watching her.

"Everything!" the bee exclaimed. "I'm so buzzy, buzzy,
buzzy, from morning to night. I have foraging to do, pollen
to collect, and a queen in the hive. I don't have time to
scratch my wing!" she said as she rubbed up against a twig
to give her wing a good scratch.

"So is that YOUR true purpose?"

"MY true purpose? When I'm so buzzy there is no time
for me. I'm just putting one wing in front of the other!
Anyway gotta fly…good luck! Buzzy, buzzy, buzzy…"
The bumblebee buzzed as she flew away.

That was it, the little caterpillar thought. I will find purpose in keeping busy. Maybe the bumblebee has a point, when you're so busy you don't have time for anything else. Hmmm, now what will my busy-ness be?

After hours of consideration the little caterpillar decided she would collect milkweed leaves from the other side of the grove, take them home, place them in a neat pile, then count them at the end of each day to see how successful she was.

And so her routine began. The little caterpillar would wake at the crack of dawn, eat a few milkweed leaves on the run, then head out to start her day of labour. She would walk across the grove, pick the leaves, walk back home and pile them neatly. Repeat. Walk across the grove, pick the leaves, walk back home and pile them neatly. Repeat.

The little caterpillar continued her new busy-ness day after day, night after night, and after a few weeks of hard labour the little caterpillar took a moment to admire her wealth.

Jo Eden Law

The little caterpillar had stockpiled towers of milkweed, which would be more than she would ever need. However, she couldn't help but wonder if it was really worth it. Her mind was bored, her body was tired and she still felt terribly glum. Not to mention she hadn't dreamt about flying in days.

Was this what she wanted from her life? A life filled with busy-ness? She could hear the fairy moth now, "All you have to do is find your true purpose and I will grant you any wish your heart desires." The little caterpillar thought, I know a life of busy-ness is not for me.

So the little caterpillar settled back into her old ways. She decided that finding her true purpose would have to wait, she couldn't let all of her hard work go to waste. And so the little caterpillar dreamt and ate, and ate and ate.

Dishonesty weakens the spirit.

"Well that looks like a feast for an army!" piped a voice out of thin air.

"I beg your pardon?"

"Attennnn-tion!" the tiny voice demanded. "Ma'am I can see how much food you have there. You need to stop eating or start sharing or it'll be the death of you!"

The bloated little caterpillar turned her head and cocked it towards the teensy weensy voice bellowing from the ground. She squinted and squinted until her eyes finally focused on a little army ant, shining in the sun like a rhinestone cowboy.

"With all due respect, ma'am, you don't look so good. Why are you gorging yourself sick?" the ant insisted.

"Haven't you heard of the motto: 'eat, drink and be merry'?" The caterpillar chuckled sarcastically.

Little Caterpillar Dreaming

"Look ma'am, you look like a nice caterpillar and all, but I have to tell you, this is no time for jokes. The last few days, while I've been on the frontline, I've seen you eating from oh eight hundred hours until oh eight hundred hours. Now don't get me wrong, I love food too, but this is lethal!" The ant raised his left eyebrow, pursed his lips, and pointed to the long and winding path of destruction the little caterpillar had chewed, chomped and left behind.

"Do you want to be zero or a hero?" the ant rallied.

"Zero or hero? I'll settle for mediocre. In any case, who do you think you are to be handing out advice?" the caterpillar sighed before she took another bite.

"I'm Sergeant Adam Ant, ma'am! At your service!" The ant stamped his feet, clicked his heels and stood at attention.

The caterpillar shrugged and shook her head in defeat. "Well, at ease Sergeant Ant, I appreciate your concern but I'm just a measly caterpillar dreaming with a pitiful purpose of ending up as someone's last supper."

The ant stared at the caterpillar in deep concern, as a frown swept his face, his voice softened. "No ma'am, with all due respect, that is absolutely not your purpose. Life is a gift meant for living. You need to dig deeper, ma'am and find your courage to follow your dreams. Don't give up. Don't give in. You can do it, I know you can."

"And how can you believe in me when I don't believe in myself?" the little caterpillar asked feebly.

Jo Eden Law

"Because I know something about courage. It's a sleeping giant that only wakes for those who persevere. It's really that simple. Set your goal, find your courage, persevere and you will wake the giant within." The ant smiled as a tear welled up in his eye, and for a few seconds the ant and the caterpillar shared a moment.

The ant then raised his hand to his temple in a respectful salute and marched off to join the army of soldiers dragging a half eaten cicada back to their queen.

Advice comes in many guises; to keep you on your path.

Little Caterpillar Dreaming

The next morning everything on the surface appeared the same: the sun rose to greet the day, the birds chirped their morning overture, the ocean waves crashed against the shore and the little caterpillar was gorging on her morning milkweed leaf. She was deeply lost in thought as the mantis skulked in the shadows.

Who am I and why am I here? She wondered.

Listening to the ant reminded the little caterpillar that there was more to her life than this. And as the little caterpillar looked up to the morning sky she saw a beautiful butterfly dance away on the breeze.

"Someday I will fly!" she avowed to the heavens.

A dark voice cackled from the murky bowels of the grove. "Did you say someday you would fly, my *petit four*?"

The little caterpillar jumped at the wicked tone.

"You are a dim little imp," the mantis alleged. "You fly? Ha! *Impossible*!"

The little caterpillar felt her hopes and dreams drain from her once again.

"I can see you still have a deplorable appetite, *Mon Cherie*! I am so pleased. But fear not, my fat little morsel, I am still waiting a little bit longer before I gobble you up. I just wanted to ensure that you were feeling miserable and afraid. It's a tastier crumb. *Au revoir*!"

And with that the mantis crept deeper within.

Jo Eden Law

The little caterpillar knew it was only a matter of course before she faced this wickedness again. And as time ticked by she continued to sweep her dreams under the milkweed.

Every day she disregarded her true purpose and continued to live in fear. She would eat enormous amounts all day long, barely able to move onto the next branch without bending it to the ground. Her attitude was also bent, she grumbled and muttered beneath her breath, becoming most unpleasant.

What used to make the caterpillar happy and content now made her bitter and annoyed. Now when she watched the butterflies soaring above she would hurl insults at them.

In fact, she had become so hardened to life that she physically felt a crust forming over her.

Night into day, day into night, the incessant voice had worn her down to a point that she couldn't take it anymore. Her breath became shallow and the pain gripped like a vice.

The milkweed branch swerved and swayed with the motion of the delirious caterpillar, causing it to buckle and twist from the unexpected movements. Then suddenly the branch cracked through the seam, forming a wooden slingshot, catapulting the little creature into the midnight sky.

What you resist, persists. – Carl Jung

PART FOUR

THE WISDOM OF A LADY

"You poor little caterpillar. You must have fallen from your branch. And I can see you are just about to molt for the final time. Well don't you worry child, Mama Ladybird is here to help!" The caterpillar felt a soft flutter against her cheek.

The caterpillar didn't know where she was; it was as though she was in a dream. She heard beautiful sounds unlike anything she had heard before, tantalising aromas tickled her bristles and when she opened her swollen eyes she saw in Technicolour.

For days, the little caterpillar was cared for and nurtured by a community of ladybirds. Soft, loving hands fed and bathed her, and a devoted choir sang and danced around her, encouraging her to find her strength to heal.

"Where am I?" she asked.

"You in paradise child."

"Am I in heaven?"

"No, child, you in Mama Ladybird land, which is the next best thing, honey!"

"What happened to me?" the little caterpillar whispered.

"Well, my girl, your story goes something like this...Your beautiful mother gave birth to you under a milkweed leaf and you were born with greatness and opportunity. However, fear and dishonestly plagued you, which led you to make easy, comfortable choices that kept you from your dreams. Time passed, you built resentment and misery, you became malicious and miserable and THEN you fell off your branch."

Mama Ladybird was right. The truth stung the little caterpillar, coiling her into a ball.

"I am hopeless!" the caterpillar cried. "I am alone, fat and lazy. I have no direction, no dreams and no purpose. I'm a complete failure."

"You're right," the ladybird said with a deadpan stare.

"Pardon?" The little caterpillar's mouth gaped open.

"I said, YOU… ARE… RIGHT… if that's what you truly believe. You see, we all have choices and what we want to believe. Your chosen thoughts have created beliefs, and this life is the result."

A fury of familiar pain and resentment roared through the caterpillar. She blurted, "How can you be so cruel! I need someone to help me, not criticize me!"

"Oh please child, don't you use that manipulative tone with me," the ladybird calmly replied. "I am trying to help you, but in order to do that YOU need to help yourself!"

The little caterpillar was stunned into silence, realizing how poorly she was behaving. And as she sat there confused, she lowered her head, closed her eyes and took a deep breath. Whilst high above the fairy moth waved her wand.

Instantly the little caterpillar's life flashed before her eyes.
She saw images of her younger caterpillar days when she
felt free, happy and alive. She saw the curious mollusc
gliding into the sun. She remembered being curious and
excited. She saw the dung beetle flash his golden smile.
She remembered Sergeant Adam Ant and the incredibly
buzzy bee. She saw the fairy moth waving her wand
and the magical daisies. Finally she saw thousands of
butterflies flit and flutter, playfully dancing around her.

Now they were calling her, speaking to her, echoing deep
within. She saw herself as a butterfly, the wind beneath her
wings, soaring through the sky. That was her dream. That
was her true purpose.

Jo Eden Law

So why did she ignore what she truly wanted and settle for a life less ordinary? Why did she decide to become resentful, bitter and angry? Why did she choose to become someone she never wanted to be?

Suddenly it all made sense. A light bulb moment.

For too long the little caterpillar had listened to the dark voice, but she had been misguided. The tears rolled down the little caterpillar's face as she reflected on her life. For quite some time they sat in silence until finally the little caterpillar spoke.

"You're right... I need to change." The little caterpillar acknowledged as she wiped the tears away.

Little Caterpillar Dreaming

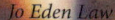

"Well hallelujah, child!" The ladybird raised her hands
to the heavens. "Can I get an A-MEN?"

"A-MEN!" the ladybird choir piped up from the gardens
as they collected aphids for their evening feast.

"Now let's get started; life doesn't wait for anyone, honey!"

The ladybird knew there was a better way for the little
caterpillar to live. She also knew their work would be
confronting and uncomfortable because she had been down
a similar road of change. She too had once lived her life
without wings.

Be true to yourself and you will find the answers.

PART FIVE

TIME TO PRAY

After a few weeks of hard work, the little caterpillar gained enough wisdom to bid the ladybird community *adieu*. It was time to embrace her new life ahead. She had learnt so much from Mama Ladybird, who was a wise old soul. So after a short but fond farewell, she embarked on her journey home.

As the little caterpillar walked along the pebbled road she reflected on her life and what an adventure it had been. She had her ups and her downs, no doubt, but she realized that every experience played an integral part in shaping her into who she was destined to be.

Keenly watching from the innards of a rotten log, the mantis waited patiently until the little caterpillar was alone, then it decided to make it's move.

The little caterpillar felt the cloak of an evil presence. She was ready. She took a long, deep breath and conjured all her strength and courage, then she turned around and found herself standing face to face with the mantis.

"The time has come, my *petit four*!" The mantis leaned forward and sung ghoulishly into her ear. "But I must say, I am quite disappointed in you. You have become a skinny, little thing, not to mention unbearably *gauche*. What happened? I was planning a delectable feast and now I am lucky to have an insipid, gritty, snack."

The caterpillar studied the boney creature as it spoke. She didn't expect it to be so gutless.

"Well, do you have any last words, you pathetic little thing?" the mantis snarled, feeling uneasy under the caterpillar's peaceful gaze.

The caterpillar took a moment to consider the frailness of the insect, and then she calmly spoke. "I must thank you." she said as she stared deep into it's alien eyes.

"Ha! *Pourquoi?* For stalking you? For mocking you? For insulting you?" the mantis spouted shifting uneasily from one leg to the other. It thought back to all the terrible things it said.

"No, I thank you because you have helped me change my life. Your hurtful comments made me search deep within myself to find out who I really am." The little caterpillar was glowing from the inside out. "I am beautiful, intelligent, strong and courageous and I have a true purpose. "

"Stupid waif. You should be begging me for mercy, not thanking me. You should be showering ME with compliments, NOT yourself. Do you NOT understand?" the mantis growled with irritation. "I AM ABOUT TO DEMOLISH YOU!"

"I am not afraid of you or your words," the little caterpillar declared confidently. She appeared to be 10 feet tall.

"You should be VERY afraid! You should!" The mantis wobbled as it watched her metamorphasize.

"Let me repeat, I am not afraid of you or your words, please leave," the little caterpillar affirmed, as she bowed her head, joined her hands in prayer and focused on her breath.

The mantis quivered at the halo of positive energy that radiated from the caterpillar as she began to meditate. It was all too much. It was so disorientated that without realizing, it too folded it's legs into a posture of prayer and bowed it's head, then it anxiously retreated into the grove. Within moments the *praying mantis* was out of sight.

Fear is afraid of the truth.

PART SIX

AWAKENING

"Where are you headed?" asked a voice from above.

The little caterpillar was wearily absorbed in thought. She had been drifting aimlessly for days.

"Have you lost your way?" the voice continued.

The little caterpillar drowsily looked up towards the heavens. The sun was so bright that all she could see was an illuminated winged figure, hovering in the sky. The caterpillar tried to speak but her mouth was too dry.

"You must be parched, you poor little thing, I have seen you wandering around for days. Here have a drink," the winged being said, then poured a sweet nectar into her mouth.

"Now, I made a promise to you. Do you remember?"

The caterpillar could barely be heard. "No, I'm sorry, my memory has gone astray."

"I know it has been a long and arduous journey, my dear little soul, and I have been there every step of the way, even when you thought I wasn't. I have seen you grow and nurture your spirit even through the darkest hours. You have persevered through your lessons and found your truth...your true purpose. You have earned your wings."

The caterpillar lay silent.

"Here, take another sip, my brave little soul."

This time the sugary drink gave the little caterpillar a surge of energy. Instinctively the caterpillar knew what had to be done and she knew it was time. She worked quickly and methodically as though something had come over her.

The little caterpillar was surrounded by an all-encompassing love. It was the most remarkable sensation that seemed incredibly familiar. It felt like home.

She weaved a small, intricate silk mat on the branch above her, then she gingerly took out her hooked hand, raised her body with all her might and attached herself to hang upside down like a fruit bat.

Little Caterpillar Dreaming

"North, South, East, West, let your spirit rise.

**Awaken the dream of belief and thought,
make haste to a winged disguise.**

**Let this caterpillar take her fate
and live a life of whole.**

**For nothing matters more in life
than the truth within one's soul."**

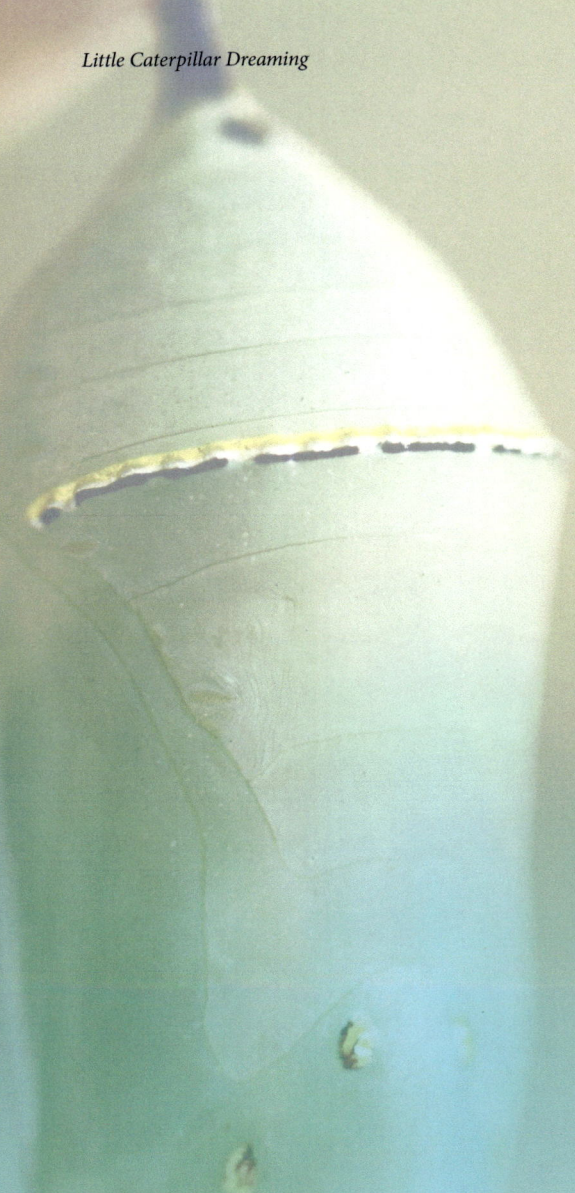

The caterpillar heard the echoes of the omnipotent chant but she was no longer awake. She released her final cloak and drifted off into a stillness within, an inner sanctuary of being, beyond ego, beyond the realm of opposites, beyond thought. A place of awakening.

Be still and know that you are and always have been.

Little Caterpillar Dreaming

Jo Eden Law

The beginning.

Thank you...

*to my angel mother, Cathy. Our journey together
will always be sacred. You are my inspiration
and you will be forever in my heart.*

*to my husband Shane Law, the love of my life. You
are the most amazing human being. Your enthusiasm,
encouragement and astute feedback (another read please?)
brought this book to fruition.*

*to Saskia Rose, for your unconditional love
and lightness of fluffy being. I love you bear.*

*to my beautiful family: Candice, Carrie, Jason and Cassidy.
Thank you for your never-never ending
love, laughter and support.*

*to my mentor and editor Stuart MacDonald for the
spirited belief that this story had potential.*

*to Getty Images and their contributing photographers
for the sensational images.*

*and finally to my fellow butterflies all over the world.
Thank you for reading this book.
I hope you enjoyed it.*

x

Author's Discussion…

This book was written with symbolic intention. An allegorical thread has been sewn through the characters and their dialogue to encourage the reader to explore the relevance and connection to their own personal journey. I have formulated a "discussion" comprising of a series of questions and annotations to encourage introspection, debate and a critical response to this story. There are no right or wrong answers since every individual will identify to the narrative differently, in accordance to our unique human experience.

PROLOUGE

p. 9 *the sky that was shrouded in a blackened veil courageously revealed its luminous truth.* Notice the personification. What does this represent?

p. 9 *And so it was, as it was always meant to be.*
Note the biblical undertone to this quote. What does this quote mean?

Discussion

PART ONE

p. 11 *The little caterpillar heard the echoes of a chant as she opened her eyes for the first time.* What is the significance of the chant? What is being implied here?

p. 11 *yet she sensed a tremendous feeling of love.* Where does this feeling come from? What does this suggest?

p. 11 Who or what does the snail symbolize or represent?

p. 12 *Yoooooou arrrrre heeeeere.* Where is 'here' and how does that relate to the life of the little caterpillar?

p. 13 *Carpe diem.* Why is this important for the caterpillar to understand?

p. 13 *a unique piece in the divine puzzle, and her life mattered beyond comprehension.* What does this mean?

p. 15 *She felt an intrinsic connection to these winged beings, and even though they looked completely different they were actually the same.* What is the significance of this 'intrinsic connection'? What is the deeper meaning?

Discussion

p. 16 Who or what does the dung beetle represent?

p. 17 *I'm a beetle of a higher orda. A sophisticated beetle on a mission.* The beetle has self proclaimed his superiority. What are the ironies in his presentation of self?

p. 17 What is the "beetle code"?

p. 18 *flicked his hand toward the caterpillar with a flagrant disreguard as he rolled his giant ball of dung away.* What is the reason for the beetle's behaviour here? What do you think the beetle believes?

p. 21 *as though an unspoken wish was granted.* Note the subtle reference to the spirituality of life.

p. 23 *Time after time she wouldn't take the leap.* Why?

p. 24 *The little caterpillar was completely absorbed by her failure.* What does this suggest about the little caterpillar at this moment? What has caused this dramatic reaction in her?

Discussion

PART TWO

p. 27 What does "The Truth in Silence" suggest?

p. 27 *standing before her was a vibrant green grasshopper majestically wrapped in an ochre coloured robe.* Who or what does the grasshopper symbolize?

p. 33 *below on a nearby branch a mantis took perch.* Who or what does the mantis symbolize or represent? Is this representative of an internal and/ or external struggle? Look carefully at how the mantis is introduced into the scenes and where it is situated during conversations.

p. 36 *I will wait and save you for a special feast, maybe my last supper.* Why do you think the mantis makes reference to "The Last Supper"? What does that tell you about the mantis?

p. 36 *The ego thrives on fallacy.* What does this mean?

p. 39 *At that very moment a luminous fairy moth frolicked above her.* Why is the timing of the arrival of the fairy moth important?

p. 39 Who or what does the fairy moth symbolize?

Discussion

p. 41 *You see, I have brought you something quite hopeful indeed.* What has the fairy moth brought the little caterpillar? How does this affect the caterpillar?

p. 43 *the vibrant daisies swayed knowingly in the breeze.* Why is this scene significant?

p. 43 *Faith is a sacred confidence in the intention of life.* What does this quote mean?

PART THREE

p. 45 Who or what does the buzzy bee symbolize?

p. 47 I don't have time to scratch my wing! She said as she rubbed up against a twig and gave it a good scratch. What does this say about the buzzy bee?

p. 48 *the little caterpillar took a moment to admire her wealth.* What does wealth mean to the little caterpillar? How would the caterpillar define success? How does this relate to modern society?

p. 51 *Dishonesty weakens the spirit.* What does this quote mean and why is it important at this point in the book?

Discussion

p. 52 Who or what does the ant symbolize or represent?

p. 57 *Advice comes in many guises; to keep you on your path.* What does this quote mean? How does it relate to the little caterpillar's entire journey?

p. 59 *Who am I and why am I here? She wondered.* What is the purpose of this introspection? What is happening within the little caterpillar?

p. 60 *And with that the mantis crept deeper within?* What does this mean?

p. 62 *She had become so hardened to life that she physically felt a crust forming over her.* What does the 'crust' represent? How does this relate to the caterpillar physically, emotionally and mentally?

p. 63 *What you resist, persists. Carl Jung.* What does this quote by Carl Jung mean?

Discussion

PART FOUR

p. 65 Who or what does the ladybird symbolize?

p. 67 *Your chosen thoughts have created beliefs, and this life is the result.* What does this quote mean and how does it influence the little caterpillar?

p. 68 *Instantly the little caterpillar's life flashed before her eyes.* Why does the caterpillar experience a life review? What does this imply?

p. 71 *Suddenly it all made sense. A light bulb moment.* What does this mean? How was the little caterpillar misguided and by whom?

p. 73 *She too had once lived her life without wings.* What does this mean in the context of the ladybird?

p. 73 *Be true to yourself and you will find the answers.* What does this quote mean?

Discussion

PART FIVE

p. 75 *she embarked on her journey home.* Where do you think the little caterpillar is going?

p. 76 *The little caterpillar felt the cloak of an evil presence. She was ready. She took a long, deep breath and conjured all her strength and courage, then she turned around and found herself standing face to face with the mantis.* Describe what the caterpillar must be thinking and feeling at this time. Who is she facing?

p. 76 *The caterpillar took a moment to consider the frailness of the insect, and then she calmly spoke. I must thank you. she said as she stared deep into it's alien eyes.* What does this confrontation suggest about the little caterpillar and her journey?

p.78-79 During the final encounter with the mantis the caterpillar metamorphosizes. How has the little caterpillar changed? Note her evolution through the story.

p. 79 *Fear is afraid of the truth.* What is the pertinence of this quote at this time?

Discussion

PART SIX

p. 81 *Where are you headed? asked a voice from above.*
Who or what does the "voice" represent?

p. 82 *Instinctively the caterpillar knew what had to
be done and she knew it was time. She worked quickly
and methodically as though something had come over her.*
What does this mean?

p. 85 *For nothing matters more in life, than the truth
within one's soul.* What does this mean?

p. 87 *The caterpillar heard the echoes of the omnipotent
chant but she was no longer awake. She released her
final cloak and drifted off into a stillness within, an inner
sanctuary of being, beyond ego, beyond the realm of
opposites, beyond thought. A place of awakening.* What is
the meaning behind this passage?

p. 87 *Be still and know that you are and always have
been.* What is the meaning behind this quote?

Thank you for your participation. I hope you have
gained an insight into the true purpose of this story.
**For further discussion and the Author's Analysis visit
www.joedenlaw.com.**

Notes…

Notes…

Notes...

Notes...

Notes...

Notes...

Notes...

Notes…

About the Author...

Jo Eden Law is the author of the upcoming series called **The Monarch Chronicles** with the release of her debut book called **Little Caterpillar Dreaming**. She lives in Australia with her husband Shane and their mystical dog Saskia Rose.

www.joedenlaw.com

Made in the USA
Monee, IL
07 July 2026

56552291R00067